OLYSLAGER AUTO LIBRARY

British Cars of the
Late Sixties 1965-1969

Compiled for the OLYSLAGER ORGANISATION
by David J. Voller

FREDERICK WARNE
London and New York

THE OLYSLAGER AUTO LIBRARY

This book is one of a growing range of titles on major transport subjects.
Titles published so far include:

The Jeep
Cross-Country Cars from 1945
Half-Tracks
Tanks and Transport Vehicles of World War 2
Armour on Wheels to 1942
Fire-Fighting Vehicles 1840–1950
Fire and Crash Vehicles from 1950
Earthmoving Vehicles
Wreckers and Recovery Vehicles
Passenger Vehicles 1893–1940
Buses and Coaches from 1940
Fairground and Circus Transport

American Cars of the 1930s
American Cars of the 1940s
American Cars of the 1950s
American Cars of the 1960s
American Trucks of the Early Thirties
American Trucks of the Late Thirties

British Cars of the Early Thirties
British Cars of the Late Thirties
British Cars of the Early Forties
British Cars of the Late Forties
British Cars of the Early Fifties
British Cars of the Late Fifties
British Cars of the Early Sixties

Motorcycles to 1945
Motorcycles and Scooters from 1945

Copyright © Olyslager Organisation BV 1982

First published 1982 by Frederick Warne (Publishers) Ltd, London

ISBN 0 7232 2897 3

Filmset and printed in Great Britain by
BAS Printers Limited, Over Wallop, Hampshire

By the turn of the decade approximately ten out of every one hundred motor cars produced worldwide was British. Offering the widest selection of models available anywhere in the world, the British Motor Industry could justifiably claim to cater both for those motorists who merely wished to conform and those who liked to be different. However, it was found to some makers cost that not all models were necessarily suitable for all export markets.

Safety in design and pollution control were increasingly becoming issues of great concern across the world, particularly in the United States of America. Dual braking systems, collapsible steering columns, child-proof door locks and simplified instrument panel layouts were very much in evidence, and the need to combat undesirable exhaust emissions was becoming a major priority for manufacturers as the imposition of strict legislation in various overseas markets threatened the acceptance of certain cars, particularly in the powerful sports car category.

British manufacturers were active in the design of exhaust emission control systems and were generally among the world's leaders in the provision of safety features in both design and equipment.

On the engine design front, many Continental manufacturers were producing light alloy power units and most favoured an overhead camshaft mechanism, whereas most British makers still preferred the conventional unit with push-rod operated valve gear, a notable exception, in the lower priced popular field, being the rear-mounted engine of the Rootes Imp range.

The period covered by this book was unquestionably exciting. Models such as the Aston Martin DBS, Jaguar XJ6, MGB GT, Ford Capri and Cortina 1600E, and, not surprisingly, the Rolls-Royce Silver Shadow were destined to become highly desirable motor cars; others such as the mid-engined Lotus Europa and the four-wheel drive Jensen FF attracted considerable interest if not for their looks, certainly for their unusual design. The arrival of the Ford Capri was especially significant because it put within the reach of the average family motorist a production car with the sort of styling which had hitherto been the preserve of more expensive, high performance, sporting models.

A selection of British cars produced during the late sixties—some well known others not so well known—is included in this book, the 28th title in The Olyslager Auto Library.

1965

UK manufacturers reached the turn of the decade on a confident but by no means complacent note. The production figures for the year were only marginally down on 1964's record output although the export quota was still below the hopes and expectations of the economists. The total production figure for the year was 1,772,045 motor cars, of which 1,069,374 were for the home market and 652,671 (38%) for export. On the design front it was very much a year for 'facelifts', the main exceptions being Austin's 1800 front-wheel drive saloon and the Reliant Motor Company's 598-cc engined Rebel, which was introduced at the small family saloon end of the market, in marked contrast to their stylish new Scimitar, which was designed to attract buyers in the more sophisticated sports coupé category.

4A Alvis 3-litre TE 21 Drophead Coupé

4B Aston Martin DB5 Convertible Volante

4A: **Alvis** 3-litre TE 21 Series III. Available in saloon and drophead coupé form, it differed from the superseded Series II, TD 21 version, mainly by twin sealed-beam headlamps set vertically in the surround, restyled rear wings, improved front suspension and steering, and increased power from its six-cylinder, 2993-cc, ohv engine. Power-assisted steering became optionally available in October 1964. The Series III was discontinued in the spring of 1967.

4B: **Aston Martin** DB5 Convertible Volante. Introduced during the summer, this variant was similar to the discontinued DB5 Convertible but identified by divided bumpers front and rear, and sidelights positioned between the flashing indicators and radiator grille. Engine power came from a six-cylinder, 3995-cc ohc unit which was coupled to a five-speed, all-synchromesh gearbox.

5A Austin Mini De Luxe Saloon

5B Austin 1800 Saloon

5C Austin A110 Westminster De Luxe Saloon

5A: **Austin** Mini. The basic and de luxe saloons and Countryman (estate) continued with a number of changes, including the introduction of Hydrolastic suspension (saloons only), a modified gearbox, diaphragm spring clutch, modified front brakes and improved instrumentation and interior appointments. Cooper and Cooper 'S' variants were also fitted with Hydrolastic suspension. Morris versions were similarly modified.

5B: **Austin** 1800 Saloon. Continuing the front-wheel drive, transverse-engine theme, this new model (ADO 17) was unveiled in the autumn of 1964. The mechanical specification included a four-cylinder, 1798-cc, ohv engine, four-speed all-synchromesh gearbox and Hydrolastic suspension. The spacious four-door body featured front and rear bench seats. Top speed was 90 mph plus. The de luxe version was fitted with overriders, carpets, hinged quarter lights, passenger sun visor and leather grab handles.

5C: **Austin** A110 Westminster De Luxe Saloon. Introduced at the beginning of the year, this version, which was in production for little more than a year, was similar to the super de luxe but was not equipped with picnic tables, walnut veneer facia or door cappings. The standard and super de luxe saloons were continued unchanged. Power for the range came from the BMC six-cylinder, 2912-cc, ohv engine.

5D: **Austin-Healey** 3000 Convertible. This powerful two/four seater sports car was continued unchanged, having been unveiled in Mk III form in February 1964. The six-cylinder, 2912-cc, 150 bhp engine gave the car impressive performance and a maximum speed in excess of 120 mph. Discontinued at the beginning of 1968 on economic grounds, largely because of its inability to meet the US Federal Safety Regulations without undergoing extensive modification.

5D Austin-Healey 3000 Mk III

6A: **Bentley** Continental. This impressive marque was now entering its last full year of production, the James Young Saloon version being discontinued in October and the H. J. Mulliner Park Ward Saloons and Convertible (shown) during the following April. The 'T' Series Bentley replaced the 'S' Series in the autumn.

6B: **Bond** Equipe GT4S. Announced in the autumn of 1964, it was mechanically similar to the superseded two plus two saloon but distinguishable by dual headlamps, restyled radiator grille, a 'clipped' rear-end giving increased luggage space and a conventional boot lid. The Mk II version of the Triumph Spitfire 1147-cc engine was fitted from the beginning of the year and wire wheels became optionally available during the summer.

6C: **Bristol** 408 Saloon. This elegant high performance model was continued unchanged. Powered by a Chrysler V-8, 5130-cc engine, it was fitted with a steel-framed, aluminium panelled coachbuilt body welded to a box-section frame and was finished to a luxury specification. Overall weight was 32 cwt. Price £4459.

6A Bentley Continental

6B Bond Equipe GT4S

6C Bristol 408 Saloon

7A: **Daimler** 2.5-litre Saloon was continued unchanged. Fitted with a V-8, 2548-cc, ohv engine and automatic transmission as standard, this model was bodily similar to the Jaguar Mk II but featured a traditional fluted radiator grille and a 'D' emblem on the wheel discs.

7B: **Daimler** 4.5-litre Limousine. First introduced in 1961, this eight-seater was basically an enlarged version of the Majestic Major. Featured a V-8, 4561-cc engine, power-assisted steering as standard, luxury trim and equipment, and a sliding glass partition. Wheelbase was 11 ft 6 in and weight $40\frac{3}{4}$ cwt.

7C: **Elva** Courier Mk IV T-Type. This open two-seater model which was first introduced by Trojan Limited of Croydon in 1963, was continued basically unchanged. Powered by either an MGB 1798-cc or Ford Cortina GT 1498-cc engine, it featured a reinforced metal and fibreglass body mounted on a ladder-type chassis. Capable of speeds around 100 mph. Price £1000 (with MGB engine), or £995 (with Ford engine).

7A Daimler 2.5-litre Saloon

7B Daimler 4.5-litre Limousine

7C Elva Courier Mk IV

8A Ford Cortina Saloon

8B Ford Cortina Lotus Saloon

8C Gordon-Keeble GK1

8A: **Ford** Cortina 113E Saloon. External changes made to this popular model included a smaller mesh radiator grille incorporating sidelamp assemblies and 'Cortina' nameplates. Other new features included front disc brakes, ventilation modifications and on de luxe models a heater and screen washers as standard. Estate car version also available. Super (118E) models were similarly modified.

8B: **Ford** Cortina Lotus 125E Saloon. This impressive performance model, powered by a 1558-cc, ohc, Lotus engine, received grille and ventilation modifications similar to the other Cortina variants. Externally distinguishable primarily by body side flashes.

8C: **Gordon-Keeble** GK1 Touring Saloon. This luxurious model continued with minor changes, including fully reclining seats and a repositioned horn button. The previously unrealistic price was raised to £3626 in February. However, the manufacturers determination to produce a luxury vehicle at a bargain basement price eventually resulted in serious financial problems and, inevitably, the voluntary liquidation of the company followed in the spring after just eighty cars had been made. The basic design was used, subsequently, by British and then American concerns in the production of a Grand Tourer.

9A: **Hillman** Imp Saloon Mk I. This 875-cc, ohc, rear-engined model, available in basic and de luxe forms, continued with a number of design improvements including manual in place of an automatic choke, incorporating a control lever located in front of the gear lever, and modified front seats.

9B: **Hillman** Super Minx. The Mk III version of this model, available in saloon and estate variants, was introduced in the summer of 1964. New features included a sharper roof line, deeper and wider windscreen, wide sloping rear window, overriders and slotted wheel trims as standard, a revised facia and reclining front seats. The estate car version had longitudinal instead of transverse roof ribs.

9C: **Humber** Hawk Series IV Saloon replaced the Series III version in the autumn of 1964 and was distinguishable from its predecessor mainly by exterior changes such as a sharper roof line, modified front and rear screens, revised rear lamp clusters, single chrome side strips and Hawk insignia. Mechanical features included a four-cylinder, 2267-cc engine and an all-synchromesh gearbox. Touring limousine and estate car models were also available.

9D: **Humber** Imperial. Introduced in the autumn of 1964, this luxuriously equipped variant, available in both saloon and limousine versions, was bodily and dimensionally similar to the contemporary Humber Super Snipe Series V, but had a black leathercloth roof covering. Discontinued in 1967.

9E: **Humber** Super Snipe Series V Saloon first appeared in the summer of 1964. Differences from the Series IV model included a squarer roof line, modified windscreen and rear window, restyled rear lamp arrangement, rubber faced overriders, Super Snipe name script, detail modifications to instrumentation and chrome surrounds to the door frames. Touring limousine and estate car versions were also available. Discontinued in 1967.

9A Hillman Imp Saloon

9B Hillman Super Minx Mk III Saloon

9C Humber Hawk Series IV Saloon

9D Humber Imperial Saloon

9E Humber Super Snipe Series V Saloon

10A Jaguar Mk 10 Saloon

10A: Jaguar Mark 10 Saloon. Introduced in the autumn of 1964. Bodily similar to the Jaguar Mark X 3.8-litre, this new model featured a six-cylinder, ohc, 4235-cc power unit and four-speed all-synchromesh gearbox. Mechanical differences from the Mark X 3.8-litre model included a redesigned radiator, improved servo-assisted brakes, modified heating system and an alternator as standard.

10B: Jaguar 'E' Type 4.2 litre Series I. Larger engined version of this classic sports car, available in open two-seater and fixed-head coupé versions. The 4235-cc engine developed 265 bhp at 5400 rpm and the car was bodily similar to the 3.8 litre model which was discontinued in the autumn. A number of modifications were also introduced on this later model including improved cooling and exhaust systems.

10C: Lotus Elan Sports. This Series 2 version was announced by the Colin Chapman stable in November 1964. Differences from the S1 included modified front brakes, restyled rear lamp clusters, full-width polished veneer facia with lockable glove box, S2 motifs and a hand brake warning light. Centre lock wheels were optionally available.

10B Jaguar 'E' Type

10C Lotus Elan Sports

11A: **MG** Midget Mk II. This popular GAN 3 Series open sports car was continued virtually unchanged—it was modified in the spring of 1964. The 1098-cc power unit developed 56 bhp at 5750 rpm.

11B: **MG** MGB (Series GHN 3). Continued with a number of detail changes including an oil cooler as standard, new type of fuel gauge, modified breathing system for the engine and a five-bearing crankshaft. The fuel tank was later enlarged to give a capacity of 12 gallons.

11C: **MG** MGB (Series GHN 3). Coune of Belgium were responsible for the coachbuilt Berlinette Coupé body shown which was mounted on a conventional MGB chassis.

11D: **Morgan** Plus Four Plus GT. This 2138-cc, 108-bhp engined Fixed Head Coupé was continued unchanged. Also available from the independent Malvern based sports car specialist were Four-Four Series V and Plus Four models, however, the Four-Four Series IV with a 1340-cc engine was discontinued.

11A MG Midget Mk II

11B MG MGB

11C MG MGB

11D Morgan Plus Four Plus GT

12A Morris Mini-Cooper 'S'

12C Morris 1100 Saloon

12B Morris Minor 1000

12A: **Morris** Mini-Cooper 'S 1275' Saloon. First introduced in March 1964, this impressive top of the range Mini was continued with a number of changes including the adoption of Hydrolastic suspension and the location of the gear lever in a rubber block insert. Output from the powerful 1275-cc engine was 76 bhp at 6000 rpm. Other Mini models continued with various changes.

12B: **Morris** Minor 1000. This popular little 1098-cc engined model, available in two- and four-door saloon, convertible and traveller versions was continued with a number of detail modifications, including improved heating system, glove box lids, two-spoke steering wheel, starter/ignition switch, oil filter warning light and crushable sun visors.

12C: **Morris** 1100 Saloon. This popular front-wheel drive model which featured a transverse engine and Hydrolastic suspension and was available with two (export only) and four doors, was continued with a number of changes including a diaphragm spring clutch, a modified gear lever and detail interior improvements. A heater became standard on de luxe versions. Austin versions were similarly modified.

13A Reliant Rebel Saloon

13B Reliant Scimitar

13C Reliant Scimitar

13A: Reliant Rebel Saloon. The Tamworth based makers of a range of popular three-wheelers and the short lived four-wheeled Sabre models were not put off by the demise of the latter and bounced back into the four-wheeled market with the announcement of two brand new models in the summer of 1964, one of which was the two-door, four seater Rebel. It featured a box section, steel chassis with fibreglass bodywork, a four-cylinder, ohv, 598-cc engine, a three-speed gearbox and trim and fittings similar to the three-wheelers. Production of this model commenced in January, by which time a number of detail changes had been made.

13B: Reliant Scimitar. The other new four-wheeler from Reliant was the Fixed Head GT Coupé which went into production in May. The Ogle-designed body shape was originally devised for a Daimler sports coupé. Features of this model were a six-cylinder, ohv, 2553-cc, 120 bhp power unit, four-speed all-synchromesh gearbox, sports coupé, fibreglass bodywork, dual headlamps and wire wheels as standard. Overall length was greater than the Sabre (14 ft v 13 ft 2 in). A ZF gearbox was optionally available. A V-6, 3-litre engine was fitted from October 1966.

13C: Reliant Scimitar. Special GTS conversion of the GT Coupé designed by David Ogle for Triplex Safety Glass Co Ltd.

14A Riley Four/Seventy Two Saloon

14B Rolls-Royce Silver Cloud

14C Rover 2000 Saloon

14A: Riley Four/Seventy Two Saloon. This four-cylinder, ohv, 1622-cc engined four-door family saloon was continued with minor modifications including a modified steering mounting, greaseless propeller shaft and a number of interior refinements. Price was £921.

14B: Rolls-Royce Silver Cloud. This superb advertisement to British engineering entered its final year of production basically unchanged. Powered by a V-8, ohv, 6230-cc engine, the model was available in numerous forms and coachbuilt body styles. The saloon, long wheelbase saloon and James Young versions were discontinued in October and the H. J. Mulliner Park Ward two and four-door saloons and the convertible the following September. The Rolls-Royce Phantom V models continued unchanged.

14C: Rover 2000 Saloon. Following its highly successful launch in the autumn of 1963, this P6 Series, four-door model was continued with a number of detail modifications including improvements to the rear suspension system, a redesigned exhaust system, improved windscreen wipers and additional interior lighting. Powered by a four-cylinder, ohc, 1978-cc engine, the model featured servo-assisted disc brakes all round and a body design which embraced many advanced safety features.

14: Singer Chamois Saloon. This latest offering from the Rootes Group was to all intents and purposes the Hillman Imp (introduced in the spring of 1963) apart from external differences such as a dummy plated front grille and additional brightwork, a number of optional extras fitted as standard and an improved interior.

14D Singer Chamois Saloon

15A: **Singer** Vogue Mk III Saloon. Announced in the autumn of 1964 this replacement for the Mk II version was distinguishable primarily by its sharper roof line, restyled windscreen and rear window and reclining front seats. Automatic transmission versions featured a floor-mounted selector lever. The Estate Car now had longitudinal instead of transverse roof ribs.

15B: **Sunbeam** Tiger Sports. This powerful two-seater tourer, which was launched onto the home market in March, featured the same body as the popular Alpine but was powered by a V-8, ohv, 4261-cc engine developing 164 bhp at 4400 rpm, dual exhaust system, servo-assisted brakes and 5.90 × 13 tyres. The Alpine Series IV model was continued with a number of modifications, including an all-synchromesh gearbox.

15C: **Triumph** Spitfire Sports. The Mk II version of this little two-seater was announced in March, production having commenced the previous December. Notable changes included increased engine power, revised exhaust manifold, diaphragm spring type clutch, improved upholstery, black leather cloth facia and door cappings and carpet kick pads. Distinguishable by a five horizontal bar radiator and Mk II emblems.

15D: **Triumph** TR4A, CTC Series, Sports Roadster and Coupé models were unveiled in March, production having started in January. New features included wider spaced horizontal radiator grille bars, sidelights relocated from grille to front wing and fitted in a chrome housing together with repeater flasher, stainless steel beading from sidelight to rear of door, wood veneer facia, handbrake located between the seats and a four-branch exhaust system with twin down-pipes.

15B Sunbeam Tiger Sports

15C Triumph Spitfire Mk II Sports

15D Triumph TR4A Sports

15A Singer Vogue Mk III Saloon

16A TVR Trident

16B Vanden Plas Princess 1100 Saloon

16C Vanden Plas Princess 4-litre 'R' Saloon

16A: **TVR** Trident. This Fiore-bodied, V-8 engined model was to mark the Company's entry into the luxury car market, but the acquisition of the assets of TVR Cars Ltd by Messrs A. and M. Lilley who then established a new company— TVR Engineering Ltd—meant that very few of these cars were ever built.

16B: **Vanden Plas** Princess 1100 Saloon. Luxurious version of the British Leyland front-wheel drive, transverse-engined family saloons which continued with a number of detail modifications. A sliding roof was optionally available.

16C: **Vanden Plas** Princess 4-litre 'R' Saloon. Introduced in the summer of 1964, it was bodily similar to the 3-litre model, which was discontinued some two months earlier, but featured smoothed tail fins, horizontal rear light units, a flatter and longer roof and fog lamps in place of horn grilles. Mechanical features included a six-cylinder, 3909-cc engine, power-assisted steering as standard and front disc brakes. The 4-litre, 3993-cc engined long-wheelbase saloon and limousine were continued unchanged, to special order only.

17A Vauxhall Viva HA SL Saloon

17B Vauxhall Victor FC 101 Saloon

17C Wolseley Hornet Mk II Saloon

17D Wolseley 16/60 Saloon

17A: Vauxhall Viva HA Series Super Luxury (SL) Saloon. Announced in the spring, this more luxurious version of the basic and de luxe saloon models, first introduced in the summer of 1963, was distinguishable by a mesh radiator grille of polished aluminium, side colour flashes, three round rear lights grouped horizontally, restyled seats, revised facia, lockable glove box and map pockets in the doors. Further changes made during the summer included amber front flashers, sidelamps incorporated in the headlamps and repositioned pedals. The basic and de luxe saloons were continued with a number of detail modifications.

17B: Vauxhall Victor FC 101 Saloon and Estate Car models superseded the FB range in the autumn of 1964. Available in basic, super (saloon only) and de-luxe versions, this Victor variant retained the four cylinder, ohv, 1595-cc engine and featured vertically-curved doors and windows, a radiator grille of five horizontal bars in a surround enclosing the headlamps, horizontal rear lamp units, concave rear window and facia instrumentation grouped in front of the driver. Powerglide automatic transmission and super-traction differential were optionally available.

17C: Wolseley Hornet Mk II Saloon. This Mini-based, 998-cc engined front-wheel drive model was continued with a number of modifications including the adoption of Hydrolastic suspension, a diaphragm spring type clutch and starter/ignition switch.

17D: Wolseley 16/60 Saloon. This sturdily built, four-door, family model was continued with a number of detail modifications. Engine power came from a four-cylinder, ohv, 1622-cc engine which developed 61 bhp at 5100 rpm. Also available was the 6/110 Mk II Saloon powered by a six-cylinder, 2912-cc engine.

1966

New model designs were certainly more in evidence than in the previous year, and much of the interest and comment centred upon the world's most famous motor car manufacturer following the announcement of their new Rolls-Royce Silver Shadow and Bentley 'T' Series models. Other interesting newcomers included the Aston Martin DB6, the front-wheel driven Triumph 1300, Vauxhall's Cresta PC and Viscount, 'E' Type 2+2 and BGT coupés from Jaguar and MG, respectively, and by no means least Jensen's four-wheel drive, FF saloon, which was announced but not actually produced until the following year, by which time it sported a new body. Production figures were down, at 1,603,679, of which 978,684 went to the home market and 624,995 (38.9%) for export.

18A: **AC** Cobra '289' Sports. Unveiled in October 1965, this later version of the Shelby inspired, two-seater road/track machine featured larger lips over the front wheel arches and more pronounced rear wheel arches, a new tubular chassis, all-round independent suspension, brake cooling slats flanking the air intake and the petrol filler relocated from the centre of the boot to the offside rear wing. Overall length was 13 ft and width 5 ft 8 in. A 7-litre engined version labelled the '427 Cobra' and sporting flared rear mudguards and alloy cast wheels was available, in the USA only, marketed by Shelby America Inc. AC also announced a 427 Convertible.

18B: **Alvis** 3-litre Series 4 TF 21 Saloon and Drophead Coupé. Destined to be the last new model to come from Alvis Limited who ceased producing private cars in the summer of 1967, this model differed from the Series III TE 21 models, which were still available in limited numbers with manual transmission only, up until the spring of 1967, mainly by increased power from the 2993-cc engine, a redesigned facia incorporating revised instrumentation, repositioned controls, electrically-heated rear window, self-adjusting handbrake and modified suspension. Automatic transmission was optionally available.

18C: **Aston Martin** DB6 Saloon. Announced in the autumn of 1965, this impressive newcomer from Aston Martin Lagonda's Newport Pagnell works was available with either the standard (282 bhp) or 'Vantage' (325 bhp) six-cylinder, 3995-cc, ohc power unit and featured a steeply raked windscreen and a higher roof and more pronounced slope back than the DB5 (1963–65). Available with either five-speed all-synchromesh or three-speed automatic transmission.

18A AC '289' Sports

18B Alvis 3-litre TF21 Saloon

18C Aston Martin DB6 Saloon

19A: **Austin** 1100 Countryman. This latest version was an estate car alternative to the highly popular saloon which continued basically unchanged. The two-door estate featured a different rear end with a top-hinged tailgate but was in most other respects identical to the saloon. Automatic transmission was available on both models.

19B: **Bentley** 'T' Series Saloon. Unveiled in the autumn of 1965, this impressive and much admired new model featured numerous significant improvements over the Series 'S' model. Shorter, lower and generally sleeker than the 'S', the new model was fitted with a steel and aluminium monocoque body and the superb technical specification included the V-8, 6230-cc engine, which incorporated minor changes, all-independent suspension embracing automatic height control, triple-circuit braking with discs all round and an advanced 'fail safe' system.

19C: **Bond** 875 Saloon. Three-wheel model powered by the Hillman Imp 875-cc engine developing 34 bhp at 4900 rpm, with a four-speed all-synchromesh gearbox. The lightweight body comprised metal sections built integrally in fibreglass reinforced plastic. Top speed was around 80 mph.

19D: **Bristol** 409 Saloon. The improvements introduced on this latest model contributed to make it a lighter and faster car than the 408, which was continued to special order only. Mechanical changes included increased engine capacity from 5130-cc to 5211-cc, an alternator in place of a dynamo, sealed cooling system, redesigned braking system, modified silencers and modified 3-speed automatic transmission. Maximum speed was in excess of 130 mph.

19A Austin 1100 Countryman

19B Bentley 'T' Series Saloon

19C Bond 875 Saloon

19D Bristol 409 Saloon

20A Ford Anglia Super Saloon

20B Ford Cortina Super Estate Car

20C Ford Corsair Saloon

20A: **Ford** Anglia 123E Super Saloon continued with minor changes, including a modified lighting arrangement. Engine power on these popular cars came from a four-cylinder, 1198-cc ohv unit. The 105E versions were similarly modified. The Anglia was discontinued in the autumn of 1967 with the advent of the Escort.

20B: **Ford** Cortina Super Estate Car Series 118E. Received a minor facelift, with chrome body strips replacing the simulated wood panelling, two-tone paint-work and 'Super' badges at the rear of the chrome strips. All Cortina models, saloons and estates, were now fitted with fixed quarter lights.

20C: **Ford** Corsair Saloon (3004E) was given a V-4, 1662-cc, ohv power unit in place of the in-line 1498-cc unit. Other changes made included Aeroflow ventilation with facia vents and extraction grilles on the rear pillars, a redesigned facia with circular instrumentation, and modifications to the braking system. Badges were now fitted centrally on the bonnet and on the boot. The GT version (3006E), powered by a V-4, 1996-cc engine, was distinguishable mainly by 'GT' badges front and rear, and the chrome strip beneath the doors. A GT Estate Car was introduced in the spring, but both GT models were discontinued in November.

20D: **Ford** Corsair Convertible. Special conversion carried out by Crayford Auto Developments Ltd, Tatsfield, Kent.

20D Ford Corsair Convertible

21A: **Ford** Zephyr Six Mk IV Saloon replaced the Mk III version early in the year. Notable differences included the V-6, 2495-cc, ohv engine, a radiator air intake below the front bumper, independent suspension all round, four-wheel servo-assisted braking system, spare wheel located in front of the engine, vents on the rear pillars, V-6 badges front and rear and a 'Zephyr' insignia between the headlamps. The car was larger all round than its predecessor. Column gear-change with a front bench seat was standard and floor change with individual front seats optional. The Zephyr Four version was similar to the 'Six' but featured a V-4, 1996-cc, ohv engine, and V-4 badges front and rear.

21B: **Ford** Zodiac Mk IV Saloon. Similar to the Zephyr Six but distinguishable mainly by horizontal bar styling between twin headlamps at the front and fluted rear panels embracing rear lamps and full width reflector. Standard specification included floor-mounted gear-change with fully reclining individual seats—column gear-change and a front bench seat were optional.

21C: **Ford** GT. Powered by a V-8, 380 bhp engine this streamlined road/track machine went into production following extensive development work in various track events, particularly on the American circuits. A Ford GT won at Le Mans in 1966.

21B Ford Zodiac Mk IV Saloon

21A Ford Zephyr Six Mk IV Saloon

21C Ford GT

22A Hillman Imp Super Saloon

22B Hillman Minx Series VI

22A: Hillman Imp Super Saloon was added to the range in the summer of 1965, coinciding with the announcement of the Mk II version of the De Luxe model; the basic model was discontinued. Distinguishing features of the super model included black side strips, mock front grille with horizontal bars and a central badge, contoured rear seats, padded arm rests and courtesy lights. Improvements also made on the de luxe model included a larger clutch, modifications to the valve mechanism and accelerator pedal, and undersealing as standard.

22B: Hillman Minx Series VI Saloon De Luxe replaced the Series V in the summer of 1965. Changes included a larger engine (1725-cc, 65 bhp, with five-bearing crankshaft) four-speed all-synchromesh gearbox, self-adjusting rear brakes, a new facia with central instrument binnacle, and identification badges on the front wings. Mk IV versions of the Hillman Super Minx Saloon and Estate Car were also available.

22C: Humber Sceptre Mk II superseded the Mk I in the summer of 1965. Notable technical changes included the 1725-cc engine, an alternator in place of the dynamo and self-adjusting rear brakes. External changes included a front grille of horizontal bars, outer headlamps set into the wings with sidelamps/flashers set into half moons above the small inner headlamps set into side grilles. Automatic transmission was optionally available.

22C Humber Sceptre Mk II Saloon

23A: Jaguar 'E' Type 4.2-litre FH Coupé 2 + 2 was unveiled in March. The model was longer (15 ft 4½ in v 14 ft 7¼ in) and higher than the two-seater FH Coupé and had a deeper windscreen. The upholstered rear seat was adjustable to give increased luggage space and a full-width parcel shelf was fitted below the facia. Automatic transmission was optionally available.

23B: Jensen C-V.8 Mk III Saloon was distinguishable from its predecessor primarily by modifications to the front end which included equal-sized dual headlamps but no chrome surround to the recess, new section bumpers (front and rear) with overriders, and separate round flashers. Other changes included a dual braking system, heater outlets to the rear foot wells, redesigned facia with face-level vents, fully reclining front seats and internal boot hinges. Manual and automatic versions were available. Replaced in the autumn by the Interceptor.

23C: Lotus Elan S3 S/E FH Coupé. Powered by the 1558-cc, ohc engine developing 115 bhp and featuring a close-ratio gearbox, servo-assisted brakes, electrically operated windows and centre lock wheels. This version, which was unveiled in the spring, was similar to the standard FH Coupé, which was introduced during the summer of 1965, but incorporated a Special Equipment package comprising additional refinements.

23D: Lotus Elan S3 S/E DH Coupé. Built to a similar specification to the S/E FH Coupé version, it featured fixed side window frames. A standard DH Coupé model was also available.

23A Jaguar 'E' Type FH Coupé 2 + 2

23B Jensen C-V.8 Mk III Saloon

23C Lotus Elan

23D Lotus Elan

24A: **MG** MGBGT Coupé Series (GHD 3). This attractive model represented a fixed head '2 + 2' alternative to the popular Roadster (GHN 3) which had been in production for more than three years. The fastback styling included a top-hinged tailgate; the occasional rear seat was padded and had a hinged squab for increasing luggage space. In most other respects the car was similar to the Roadster, which was continued unchanged. An anti-roll bar became standard on both versions later in the year.

24B Morgan Plus Four Competition

24A MG MGBGT Coupé

24B: **Morgan** Plus Four Competition Two-Seater added to the Malvern stable in the autumn of 1965. Appearance was improved by a lowered bonnet line, and new features included a four-branch exhaust manifold, wire wheels with wide-base tyres and adjustable rear shock absorbers. Price was £938.

24C: **Morris** 1800 Saloon. Introduced in March, this Morris version was virtually identical to the 1798-cc transverse-engined Austin apart from the front grille which comprised six horizontal bars and a circular Morris badge. Standard and de luxe models were available. Notable mechanical features included a four-speed all-synchromesh gearbox and Hydrolastic suspension.

24C Morris 1800 Saloon

25A Riley Kestrel 1100 Saloon

25B Rolls-Royce Silver Shadow Saloon

25C Rover 3-litre Mk III Saloon and Coupé

25A: Riley Kestrel 1100 Saloon. Added to the popular 1100 range in the autumn of 1965, this version was powered by a twin-carburettor version of the 1098-cc transverse engine and easily distinguishable by a traditional Riley radiator grille and narrow side grilles incorporating front lamp units. The interior was finished to a higher specification than the Austin and Morris versions, and featured a walnut veneer facia with round instrument dials.

25B: Rolls-Royce Silver Shadow Saloon. Introduced along with the 'T' Series Bentley, it was identical apart from the radiator grille which although unmistakably Rolls-Royce was, nevertheless, shallower than on previous models. In keeping with tradition, the R-R specification included numerous outstanding features such as a triplicated hydraulic braking system, improved power-assisted steering and automatic height control.

25C: Rover 3-litre Mk III Saloon and Coupé. Bodily similar to the Mk II, which was discontinued at the beginning of the year, but featuring full-length body side strips, name flashes on the front wings and boot-lid, larger front badge, heating system extended to the rear compartment, restyled front seats and individual rear seats.

26A: **Singer** Chamois Mk II Saloon. Replacement for the Mk I in September 1965, it featured a number of changes including modifications to the engine (valves and choke mechanism), contoured rear seats, padded front and rear parcel shelves, undersealing as standard and Mk II plaques on doors.

26B: **Singer** Gazelle Series VI Saloon differed from its predecessor by significant changes such as a larger engine (1725-cc) with five-bearing crankshaft and self-adjusting rear brakes, and various external modifications including the adoption of a squat grille flanked by side grilles comprising three horizontal bars, restyled lamp units and emblems on the front wings.

26C: **Singer** Vogue Series IV Saloon and Estate Car. In common with the other Rootes medium range models the latest Vogues were given a 1725-cc, five-bearing crankshaft engine which developed 85 bhp at 5500 rpm, self-adjusting rear brakes and quarter vent locks. Other modifications included an alternator in place of the generator, chrome surrounds to the headlamps, a chrome 'V' on the front wings and '1725' emblems.

26A Singer Chamois Saloon

26B Singer Gazelle Series VI Saloon

26C Singer Vogue Series IV Saloon

27A: Sunbeam Rapier Series V Saloon. Modified in line with the other medium range Rootes models, it was now powered by the 1725-cc, five-bearing crankshaft, 85 bhp engine, and featured a twin exhaust manifold, self-adjusting brakes, an alternator replacing the generator, quarter vent locks and '1725' emblems.

27B: Sunbeam Alpine Series V Sports Tourer and GT Hardtop. Incorporated most of the Rootes medium range model modifications including a more powerful version of the 1725-cc engine which developed 95.5 bhp at 5500 rpm and was fitted with twin Zenith-Stromberg carburettors. Also featured a number of detail changes. The V-8 engined Tiger was continued unchanged.

27C: Triumph 1300 Saloon. New small family four-door model powered by a front-wheel driven 1296-cc engine which developed 61 bhp at 5000 rpm and was based on the Herald's 1147-cc unit. Externally resembling the general styling of the larger '2000', the new model featured all-round independent suspension, all-synchromesh gearbox, front disc brakes, an eight horizontal bar front grille with single headlamps and an interior which was finished to a high standard for a car priced at just under £800.

27D: Triumph 2000 Estate Car. Mechanically identical to its saloon counterpart, apart from heavy duty springs, different tyres and a repositioned fuel tank, this latest addition to the Triumph range featured a top-hinged, counterbalanced tailgate. This gave access to a carpeted luggage compartment which could be increased by folding down the rear seat squab. The overall length was the same as the saloon, which continued with minor modifications. Automatic transmission and power-assisted steering were optionally available.

27A Sunbeam Rapier Series V Saloon

27C Triumph 1300 Saloon

27B Sunbeam Alpine Series V

27D Triumph 2000 Estate Car

28A Vauxhall Viva De Luxe '90' Saloon

28C Vauxhall Bedford Beagle Mk II Estate Car

28B Vauxhall Viva SL '90' Saloon

28A/B: **Vauxhall** Viva HA De Luxe '90' and SL '90' Saloons. High performance models added to the Viva range in the autumn of 1965. A raised compression ratio, twin intake air-cleaner and Stromberg carburettor were features of the '90's' more powerful engine, which developed 60 bhp compared with 50 bhp of the standard unit. Other differences included a stronger propeller shaft, revised instrumentation, servo-assisted front disc brakes and twin tone horns.

28C: **Vauxhall** Bedford Beagle Estate Car. First introduced in the summer of 1964, this conversion by Martin Walter of Kent on a 8-cwt Viva van appeared in Mk II form in the autumn of 1965 with a number of detail changes, the most noticeable being coloured side flashes on the body.

29A Vauxhall Cresta PC Saloon

29A: **Vauxhall** Cresta PC Saloon. Replacement for the PB (the Velox label was now dropped), this new model announced in the autumn of 1965 came in standard and de luxe versions. The body which gave the car more interior space than its predecessor was styled on American lines with an upswept waistline over the rear wheels. The six-cylinder, 3294-cc engine was uprated with higher-life camshafts, modified valve springs and a different carburettor, and a three-speed manual gearbox was standard; four-speed manual and three-speed automatic were optional. The standard version featured single headlamps and the de luxe version dual headlamps.

29B: **Vauxhall** Viscount Saloon. This new four-door model was bodily similar to the Cresta PC De Luxe but distinguishable by a black-grained fabric covered roof, a mesh radiator grille and a luxury specification which included, as standard, Powerglide automatic transmission, power-assisted steering, electrically-operated windows and a heated rear window. Price was £1483. Four-speed manual transmission was optionally available.

29C: **Wolseley** 1100 Saloon. This model joined MG, Riley and Vanden Plas at the luxury end of 1100 market in the autumn of 1965. Powered by a twin-carburettor version of the 1098-cc transverse engine, it was distinguishable mainly by the traditional Wolseley front grille. The interior finish was to a high standard and included walnut veneer facia and door cappings.

29B Vauxhall Viscount Saloon

29C Wolseley 1100 Saloon

30A AC 428 Convertible

1967 Although a somewhat gloomy year in terms of actual output, with overall production figures some 200,000 down on 1965's results, there were some interesting developments both in terms of new model design and the updating of existing models to meet the demand for increased engine power, more interior space and added refinement. AC with their 428 Convertible and Jensen with the Interceptor and a new body for their recently introduced FF Saloon caught the eye in the specialist luxury sports car market, whereas Rootes with their Hunter-bodied models and Ford with the Mk II Cortinas received most attention in the popular, medium range saloon car market. Other newcomers included the Lotus Europa, for export only, and Elan Plus 2, Triumph GT6 and Vauxhall Viva HB range. Overall production for the year was 1,522,013, of which 988,273 were for the home market and 563,740 (36.3%) for export. A famous name disappeared when Alvis cars were discontinued during the summer.

30A: **AC** 428 Convertible. Larger engined replacement for the stylish 427 Convertible (1965–66), it was introduced in October 1966 and joined by an equally attractive Fastback Coupé version the following March. The lightweight body was designed by Frua of Italy and mounted on an extended '289' chassis; engine power was delivered by a massive V-8, 7017-cc (428 cu in), 345 bhp unit from Ford in the States. Initially, production involved shipping the chassis to Italy for the all-steel body to be welded on. The complete shell was then returned to Thames Ditton for trimming and painting. The luxury specification included silver enamelled wire wheels, electrically-operated windows, black leather trim and a wood rim steering wheel.

30B: **Aston Martin** Volante Convertible. Mounted on the DB6 chassis, this soft-top alternative to the DB6 Saloon featured a power-operated hood, square-cut rear end styling with modified rear lamp units and divided 'wrap-around' bumpers at the front.

30C: **Austin** 1800 Saloon. Continued with a number of changes including piled carpets, walnut veneer facia, centre console and door cappings, and revised heater controls. Seat trim on de luxe versions now featured Ambla instead of hide. Power-assisted steering became optionally available later in the year.

30B Aston Martin Volante Convertible

30C Austin 1800 Saloon

31A: **Austin-Healey** Sprite Mk IV. Now featured a larger engine (Mini-Cooper based twin carburettor, 1275-cc unit in place of the 1098-cc unit of the Mk III), different clutch, separate clutch and brake hydraulic master cylinders and an integral, non-removable folding hood.

31B: **Bond** Equipe GT 4S 1300 Sports Saloon. Mechanically different from the superseded GT 4S model mainly by the introduction of a 1296-cc, 75 bhp Triumph engine, this model also featured revised styling and improved fibreglass bodywork.

31C: **Bond** Equipe GT 2-litre Sports Saloon. This attractive four-seater was mounted on the chassis, and featured the six-cylinder, 1998-cc engine and gearbox, of the Triumph Vitesse. The body included twin headlamps located in a recessed, full-width radiator grille, and a large, flat, electrically-heated rear screen. Interior accommodation comprised front bucket seats adapted from those of the new Triumph GT6 model and the rear bench seat of the Vitesse. Price £1095.

31D: **Daimler** Sovereign Saloon. Although using the shell of the Jaguar 'S', this new model was distinguishable by its modified front end featuring the traditional fluted radiator grille, twin headlamps, with separate sidelamps and wrap-around indicators, and air intakes either side of the grille. The 4.2-litre XK Jaguar engine was paired with either a new all-synchromesh gearbox with overdrive, or Borg Warner, automatic transmission. The impressive technical specification included power steering, dual hydraulic braking, independent suspension all round; and the luxurious interior included leather hide upholstery and selective interior temperature control.

31B Bond Equipe GT4S 1300 Sports Saloon

31C Bond Equipe GT 2-litre Sports Saloon

31A Austin-Healey Sprite Mk IV

31D Daimler Sovereign Saloon

32A Fairthorpe TX-GT

32B Ford Cortina De Luxe Saloon

32C Ford Cortina Lotus Sports Saloon

32A: **Fairthorpe** TX-GT. This lightweight sports car from the Buckinghamshire based manufacturer was evolved from the prototype TX1 which was first exhibited at the 1965 London Motor Show. Powered by a six-cylinder, 1998-cc engine, which was available in various stages of tune, the car featured a Torix Bennett designed two-door, fibreglass body with opening rear window. The specification included wire wheels, leather upholstery, reclining seats and full instrumentation. Available fully assembled or in kit form.

32B: **Ford** Cortina De Luxe Saloon. Mk II replacement for the original Cortina, this latest model, available in two-and four-door versions, featured a redesigned body with more rounded styling and a full-width radiator grille of horizontal bars incorporating single headlamps and sidelamp/flasher units. The standard engine was a four-cylinder, five bearing crankshaft 1298-cc, 53.5 bhp unit; the 1500-cc, 61 bhp engine, was optionally available. Other changes included a diaphragm spring clutch and modifications to the suspension. Super (1500-cc, 61 bhp engined) and GT (1500-cc, 78 bhp engined) versions were also available. 1300 and 1500 Estate Car models became available in February.

32C: **Ford** Cortina Lotus Sports Saloon (3020E Series). Added to the Mk II range in March, this high performance replacement for the earlier 125E Series model was similar in appearance to the Cortina GT, apart from a black radiator grille and, where applicable, optional body side flashes. Powered by the 1558-cc, ohc, 110 bhp Lotus engine.

33A Ford Corsair 2000E Saloon

33B Ford Zephyr Four Mk IV Estate Car

33A: Ford Corsair 2000E Saloon.
Distinguishable from the 2000 saloon and estate
car, which replaced the Corsair GT models at the
end of 1966, mainly by a radiator grille
comprising seven horizontal bars and a 'V'
badge, black vinyl roof, horizontal strip across
the boot bearing the name, no chrome side
strips, twin reversing lamps as standard and full-
width walnut veneer facia. The centre console
was padded to form an armrest between the
reclining front seats. Corsair (1662-cc engined)
saloons were continued basically unchanged
apart from the introduction of a new gearbox.

33B: Ford Zephyr Four Mk IV Estate Car.
Announced in the autumn of 1966, this
conversion was carried out by E. D. Abbott and
Co. of Farnham, Surrey. The top-hinged
counterbalanced tailgate gave access to a fully-
carpeted luggage area which, with the rear seat
folded flat, could stow 70 cu ft of luggage. A
Zephyr Six version was also available.

33C: Ford Executive Saloon. Introduced during
the autumn this model was, essentially, a de luxe
version of the Zodiac Mk IV. The technical
specification included, as standard, automatic
transmission and power-assisted steering. Other
distinguishing features included a sun-roof,
walnut facia, chrome strips below the doors and
a star badge on the front grille.

33C Ford Executive Saloon

34A Hillman California FH Coupé

34B Hillman Husky Estate Car

34C Hillman Hunter Saloon

34A/B: Hillman Californian FH Coupé and Husky Estate Car. Two new variants of the Imp which were basically similar to their saloon counterpart except for obvious body styling and associated accommodation and luggage space differences. The Singer Coupé version, the Chamois, was similar to the Californian but more luxuriously equipped.

34C: Hillman Hunter Saloon. New model unveiled in the summer/autumn of 1966 and featuring a flush-sided, clean-lined body shape which was adopted for all Rootes medium range saloon cars during that period and remained basically unchanged until Singer and ultimately the Hillman, Humber and Sunbeam makes were dropped in the mid-seventies. Powered by the four-cylinder, 1725-cc engine (a 1496-cc unit was optionally available) the four-door Hunter featured a full-width radiator grille of horizontal bars incorporating single headlamps. Overall length was 14 ft $1\frac{1}{2}$ in. Overdrive and automatic transmission were optionally available.

34D: Hillman Minx Estate Car and Saloon. Were similar to the Hunter but powered by the 1496-cc engine when fitted with the standard manual synchromesh gearbox or the 1725-cc unit with the optional automatic transmission. The overall length of the estate, which was fitted with a top hinged tailgate, was slightly greater than the saloon.

34D Hillman Minx Estate Car

35A Jaguar 420 Saloon

35B Jaguar 420G Saloon

35C Jensen FF Saloon

35D Jensen Interceptor Saloon

35A: **Jaguar** 420 Saloon. Introduced in the summer of 1966 this four-door model was similar in appearance to the S-type but featured dual headlamps. It was externally distinguishable from the Daimler Sovereign mainly by the different radiator and badges. The two cars were almost identical, technically, except that power-steering and overdrive were standard on the Sovereign and optional on the 420.

35B: **Jaguar** 420G Saloon. This model was generally similar in appearance to the Mark 10 which it replaced, but was distinguishable by full length chrome side strips, heavier vertical bar at the centre of the radiator grille and repeater flashers mounted on the front wings. The mechanical specification was generally similar to that of the Mk 10 with engine power coming from the six-cylinder, 4.2 litre, ohc unit which developed 255 bhp at 5400 rpm. A Limousine version was also available.

35C: **Jensen** FF Saloon. Although originally announced in October 1965 with a body similar to the C-V.8, this revolutionary newcomer was not in fact produced until October 1966, by which time it sported a purposeful new body styled and constructed by Italian coachbuilder Vignale. The FF ('Ferguson Formula') boasted a four-wheel drive system, the 6.2-litre, 330 bhp Chrysler engine with Torqueflite automatic transmission, anti-lock braking system, power-assisted steering and hide upholstery. The production body featured a huge wrap-around rear screen, twin side-by-side headlamps and a radiator grille of horizontal bars. Price was £5340.

35D: **Jensen** Interceptor Saloon. This replacement for the C-V.8 featured basically the same handsome, coachbuilt body shell from Vignale of Italy as the 're-bodied' FF model, the main differences being that the FF had a brushed metal roof pan, a bonnet air scoop, twin extractor vents behind the front wheel arches and 'FF' insignia front and back. Powered by the V-8, 6276-cc ohv engine, the Interceptor was available with either manual or automatic transmission, was some three inches shorter than the FF and had a top speed in the region of 140 mph. Price £3743.

36A Lotus Europa S2 FH Coupé

36B Lotus Elan Plus 2 FH Coupé

36C MG Midget Mk III Sports

36A: Lotus Europa S2 FH Coupé. Although released for overseas markets, it was not officially introduced in the UK until the summer of 1969. A somewhat revolutionary model which featured a four-cylinder, 1470-cc, ohv, midship-mounted engine and an unusual one piece, fibreglass body with recessed headlamps and large fins extending from the roof line to the rear end.

36B: Lotus Elan Plus 2 FH Coupé. Spring saw the arrival of this new, two plus two model which was basically a 'stretched' version of the S3 two-seater FH Coupé, the extra accommodation coming from occasional rear seats. The output of the 1558-cc, ohc engine was increased to 118 bhp and the model also featured servo-assisted disc brakes all round and Airflow ventilation. The overall length was some two feet greater than the two-seater FH Coupé.

36C: MG Midget Mk III (G/AN4 Series). This popular sports car was given the same modifications as the Austin-Healey Sprite Mk III, but was distinguishable basically by its distinctive radiator grille and badges. The 1275-cc engine developed 64 bhp at 5800 rpm.

36D: Morgan Plus 4 Tourer. The two-seater version was given a lowered bonnet line at the end of 1966 to bring it into line with other models in the Morgan range. All other Plus 4 and 4/4 Series V models were continued unchanged, although the Plus 4 Plus GT FH Coupé was discontinued.

36E: Riley Elf Mk III Saloon. Differences from the superseded Mk II included concealed door hinges, winding windows, push-button door handles, remote-control gear lever and fresh-air vents at each end of the facia. All Riley production ceased in the summer/autumn of 1969, by which time the Mk III Elf had been given reclining front seats, and an all-synchromesh gearbox, as standard; automatic transmission was optionally available from October 1967.

36D Morgan Plus 4 Four-Seater Tourer

36E Riley Elf Mk III Saloon

37A Singer Gazelle Saloon

37B Singer Vogue Estate Car

37C Sunbeam Imp Sport

37D Sunbeam Tiger Mk II Sports

37A: Singer Gazelle Saloon. Fitted with the new body shell of the Hillman Hunter, this version was externally recognizable mainly by its different front end treatment incorporating rectangular headlamps and chrome waistline beading. Powered by the 1496-cc engine as standard; the 1725-cc unit was fitted with the optional automatic transmission. The Vogue version was better equipped, generally, included the 1725-cc engine as standard and featured dual headlamps.

37B: Singer Vogue Estate Car. Similar to the Hillman Minx Estate but equipped more in line with the Vogue Saloon, the model had a top-hinged tailgate which gave access to generous luggage space, with the rear seat folded flat. The Vogue and the Vauxhall Viva HB were the first British built cars to be fitted with rectangular headlamps. Initially fitted with a 73 bhp version of the 1725-cc engine, but later given the 80 bhp unit of the saloon.

37C: Sunbeam Imp Sport. More powerful version of the Imp based saloon, it featured a twin-carburettor version of the 875-cc engine which developed 55 bhp, louvres in the rear engine compartment lid, special wheel trims, servo-assisted brakes and reclining front seats. From May there was zero camber on the front wheels. The Singer Chamois Sport was similar.

37D: Sunbeam Tiger Mk II Sports. This model was aimed at the export market but sadly ceased production barely six months after its announcement. Differences from the Mk I included a V-8, 4737-cc, 200 bhp engine, honeycomb radiator grille, broad body side flashes and additional brightwork. Reversing lamps were fitted as standard.

38A Triumph Spitfire Mk III Sports

38C Triumph GT6 FH Coupé

38B Triumph Vitesse 2.0 litre Saloon

38D Triumph 2000 Saloon

38A: **Triumph** Spitfire Mk III Sports. Larger engined version of this two-seater, which featured a number of changes including a modified front end incorporating a wider radiator grille, raised rear bumpers, a veneer facia with black surround and reversing lamps as standard. The 1296-cc, ohv engine developed 75 bhp at 6000 rpm.

38B: **Triumph** Vitesse 2.0-litre Saloon. Larger engined replacement for the Vitesse, distinguishable mainly by emblems front and rear, reversing lights and a three-spoke leather trimmed steering wheel. Technical changes included a larger diaphragm spring clutch and improved brakes.

38C: **Triumph** GT6 FH Coupé. Based on the body and chassis of the Spitfire, this new sports two-seater was powered by a six-cylinder, 1998-cc, ohv, 95 bhp engine and the bodywork featured a radiator grille of five horizontal bars, a dipping waistline, a bonnet power bulge and a sloping roof with top-hinged tailgate. Top speed was in excess of 105 mph.

38D: **Triumph** 2000 Saloon and Estate Car continued with a number of changes including black rubber inserts in the overriders, full-flow ventilation with external ducts over the rear window on the saloon and below the tailgate window on the estate, and perforated leather seats.

39A Vauxhall Viva HB Saloon

39B Vauxhall Brabham Viva De Luxe '90' Saloon

39D Vauxhall Cresta PC Estate Car

39C Vauxhall Victor FC 101 Estate Car

39E Wolseley 18/85 Saloon

39A: Vauxhall Viva HB Saloon. Introduced in the summer of 1966, this replacement for the HA featured an all new body with a flattened nose, swept-up waistline and curved side panels. The engine was a bored-out, 1159-cc version of the previous unit, and in standard form developed 47 bhp at 5400 rpm. The optional tuned version developed 60 bhp. The mechanical specification also included a redesigned suspension system. The HB range comprised five models ranging in price from £579 to £708.

39B: Vauxhall Brabham Viva De Luxe '90' HB Saloon. Developed by the Australian world champion racing driver Jack Brabham, this sports saloon was easily distinguishable from other models in the Viva range by distinctive body flashes and Brabham badges front and rear. An SL'90' version was also available. The twin-carburettor '90' engine developed 79 bhp.

39C: Vauxhall Victor FC 101 Estate and Saloon Car. Modifications made to model included a restyled radiator grille incorporating the nameplate, chrome beading along the waist and wings and on Super versions a heater as standard. The FC series, including the VX4/90 version, was discontinued in the summer.

39D: Vauxhall Cresta PC Estate Car. Announced in January, this conversion by Martin Walter Limited of Folkestone, Kent was available for little more than twelve months.

39E: Wolseley 18/85 Saloon. March marked the arrival of this new model which was a variant of the Austin 1800. Powered by a front wheel driven, 1798-cc engine which developed 84 bhp at 5300 rpm, it was recognizable by the traditional grille flanked by three horizontal bars each side, chrome strips along the rear wings and boot lid, and reversing lamp built into the rear bumper. Interior finish and fittings were to a high standard and included a walnut facia. Power steering was fitted as standard, and automatic transmission was optionally available.

1968

An interesting crop of new models and encouraging production figures which promptly halted the downward slide of the previous year gave cause for optimism as the British Motor Industry moved towards the end of the sixties. It was the eagerly awaited small car from Ford in the shape of the new Escort which received most publicity and soon gained a vote of approval from press and public alike. MG attempted to uprate their MGB package with the introduction of a companion model—the six-cylinder engined MGC. Other new arrivals included the Triumph 13/60, TR5 PI and 2.5 PI, the Sunbeam Rapier and Stiletto, the Austin 3.0 litre and Vauxhall's FD range, 1,815,936 cars were produced during the year, 1,013,163 of which were for the home market and 802,773 (44%) for export.

40A: **Aston Martin** DBS-6 Sports Saloon. Introduced in October 1967, this addition to the range was powered by the 3995-cc engine, and the technical specification included a five-speed gearbox and de Dion rear suspension with inboard rear brakes. The works designed two-door fastback body featured twin headlamps, and vents to the rear of the front wheel arches and on the rear pillars. The DB6 Saloon and Volante Convertible continued unchanged.

40B: **Austin** Mini 1000 Saloon Super De Luxe and Countryman. Added to the Mini range, which was designated Mk II from October 1967. The 998-cc engine, as used in the Riley Elf and Wolseley Hornet, developed 38 bhp at 5250 rpm. Externally the Mk II was recognizable from its predecessor mainly by a new front grille comprising eleven horizontal bars, and on the saloon, a wider rear window and modified rear lamp clusters. Mini 850 models were similarly facelifted. All super de luxe models were finished to a better specification which included hinged quarter lights, carpets and a heater as standard. An all-synchromesh gearbox was introduced during the summer.

40C: **Austin** Mini Moke. Mechanically similar to the Mk II Mini Saloon but fitted with a detuned 848-cc engine and 'dry' rubber cone suspension. The open body was fitted with a vinyl-treated fabric tilt cover, the bonnet could be detached from its hinges and the windscreen either folded down or removed. Passenger seat and rear seats were optional. Production of the Mini Moke was transferred to Australia in 1969.

40A Aston Martin DBS-6 Sports Saloon

40B Mini Range

40C Austin Mini Moke

41A: **Austin** Mini-Cooper 'S 1275' Saloon. Appeared in Mk II form in the autumn of 1967. Facelifted generally in line with the less powerful Minis, however, the front grille differed by having seven thick horizontal bars, and a 'Mk II 1275' designation was mounted at the rear. An all-synchromesh gearbox was fitted during the summer. A Mini-Cooper '1000' model was also available.

41B: **Austin** 1100 Mk II Saloon and Countryman. Given a facelifted exterior and numerous detail changes during the autumn of 1967. Distinguishable by the restyled front grille and rear designation, and on saloon versions, by reshaped tail fins and larger rear lamp clusters. The central instrument panel was wood finished, with round speedometer and rocker switches; Super de Luxe and Countryman models had additional brightwork and a full-width facia in silver with a strip type speedometer. The Countryman featured simulated wood body side strips. Morris versions were similarly facelifted.

41C: **Austin** 1300 Mk II Countryman and Saloon. Larger engined models added to the range, were basically similar in appearance to the Mk II 1100 but the front grille featured four horizontal twin bars and a '1300' designation was mounted at the rear. The four cylinder, 1275-cc, ohv engine developed 60 bhp at 5250 rpm and the mechanical specification included an all-synchromesh gearbox. De luxe and super de luxe versions of the saloon were available, initially, but the de luxe models were discontinued in February. Morris versions were also available.

41D: **Austin** 1800 Mk II De Luxe Saloon. Facelifted and more powerful successor to the previous model, it was recognizable by a front grille of four horizontal twin bars with intermittent vertical bars and a centre badge, extended rear wings incorporating vertical rear lamp units, rear identification and larger wheels. The output of the 1798-cc engine was increased, initially to 81 bhp and subsequently to 86 bhp.

41A Austin Mini-Cooper 'S 1275' Saloon

41B Austin 1100 Mk II Saloon

41C Austin 1300 Countryman

41D Austin 1800 Mk II Saloon

42A Austin 3-litre Saloon

42B Bentley 'T' Series Saloon

42A: **Austin** 3-litre Saloon. Top of the range model, which was unveiled in the autumn of 1967. The four-door body was larger than the 1800 and featured a full-width radiator grille with rectangular headlamps and at the rear rounded fins incorporating vertical lamp units. The technical specification included a six-cylinder, 2912-cc engine (as fitted in the A110 Westminster which was discontinued in January), Hydrolastic suspension with auto levelling at the rear and power-assisted steering. The luxurious interior included a walnut veneer facia, leather upholstery and reclining front seats. Later versions had twin round headlamps.

42B: **Bentley** 'T' Series. The four-door Standard Saloon and two-door H. J. Mulliner Park Ward Saloon were continued and from June were given an anti-roll bar and stiffened dampers. September 1967 saw the addition of the H. J. Mulliner Park Ward Drophead Coupé which featured a power-operated hood.

42C Bristol 410 Saloon

42C: **Bristol** 410 Saloon. Whilst retaining the basic shape of the 409, the new car was distinguishable mainly by the front end being recessed round the headlamps, full length double chrome side strips, smaller wheels and restyled wheel trims. Technical changes included power steering, now fitted as standard, a floor-mounted gear selector replacing the push-button selector for the automatic transmission, and two separate hydraulic braking systems. Replaced by the 411 in the autumn of 1969.

42D: **Daimler** V-8 250 Saloon. Improved version of the 2½-litre model, and recognizable primarily by slimmer bumpers and the rear insignia. It now featured as standard, a heated rear window, reclining front seats, an alternator, ventilated upholstery and padded door cappings and facia. The model was discontinued in 1969.

42D Daimler V-8 250 Saloon

43A Ford Escort De Luxe Saloon

43B Ford Escort Twin Cam Saloon

43C Ford Cortina Super Estate Car

43A: **Ford** Escort Saloon. Announced at the beginning of the year this new 'small car' replacement for the Anglia featured a low two-door body with 'swept-up' waistline and a full-width radiator grille of four horizontal and ten vertical bars flanked by single headlamps. Available with either a 1098-cc, ohv, 49 bhp engine (1100 Basic, De Luxe and Super models) or 1298-cc, ohv, 58 bhp engine (1300 Super model). A 1300 GT version was also available and featured higher engine output, a close-ratio gearbox, servo-assisted brakes and fuller instrumentation. De luxe estate cars were introduced in the early spring. Automatic transmission became optionally available on super models in May.

43B: **Ford** Escort Twin Cam Saloon. Similar to the 1300 GT but powered by a 1558-cc, ohc, twin-carburettor, 109.5 bhp engine and gearbox (as used in the Cortina Lotus) and externally distinguishable by a black matt radiator grille, flared wheel arches and front quarter bumpers. Highly successful on the rally and track racing circuits, it had impressive performance and accelerated from 0 to 60 mph in less than 9 seconds.

43C: **Ford** Cortina Super Estate Car. Modifications introduced in the summer of 1967 included new 'cross-flow' headed 1298-cc and 1598.8-cc engines using 'bowl in piston' combustion chambers to replace the original 1298-cc and 1500-cc units. The new engines developed 58 bhp at 5000 rpm and 71 at 5000 rpm, respectively. The de luxe version and saloon variants were similarly modified. A GT estate car was available to special order only.

43D: **Ford** Cortina 1600E Saloon. Luxuriously equipped ('Executive') sporting model which was distinguishable externally, mainly by a matt black radiator grille, wide rim sculptured wheels and badges on rear pillar and boot lid. Powered by the 1598.8-cc engine fitted in the Cortina GT, the impressive standard specification included lowered suspension, reversing lamps, twin driving lamps, painted coach-line, reclining front seats, polished wood facia and door cappings, cut pile carpets and a padded centre console.

43D Ford Cortina 1600E Saloon

44A Ford Zephyr Six Mk IV De Luxe Saloon

44B Gilbern Genie

44A: Ford Zephyr Six Mk IV De Luxe Saloon and Estate Car. An addition to the range, it featured a full-width radiator grille with centre star badge, raised motif on the bonnet, larger wheels, floor gear shift, bucket seats and luxurious upholstery. Zephyr Four Mk IV De Luxe saloon and estate car models were also available, to a similar specification. Zodiac and Executive models continued with a number of changes.

44B: Gilbern Genie. Replacement for the earlier GT model, this attractive sports saloon from the Welsh specialist manufacturer featured a Ford V-6, 2994-cc engine and four-speed, all-synchromesh gearbox, MGB brakes, suspension and rear axle, and a fibreglass body which was rather less 'boxy' than its predecessor. Top speed was approximately 120 mph and price £1917 (£1447 in kit form). A Genie-based petrol injection model was introduced in the spring of 1969.

44C: Hillman Hunter Mk II Saloon. Distinguishable from the original model by a cross mesh black radiator grille with central badge and chrome surround, rectangular headlamps and a grey instead of black facia. Servo-assisted brakes were introduced initially as an option and later as standard. Shown is the Rootes entered car on the 1968 London/Sydney Marathon crewed by Andrew Cowan (left), Colin Malkin (right) and Brian Coyle.

44C Hillman Hunter Mk II Saloon

45A Humber Sceptre Saloon

45B Jaguar 240 Saloon

45C Lotus Elan S4 FH Coupé

45D Marcos Mini

45E Marcos 1500

45A: Humber Sceptre Saloon. Luxurious addition to the 'Hunter' bodied Rootes range, it featured a radiator grille of nine horizontal bars flanked by twin headlamps, black vinyl roof with an emblem on the rear pillar, horizontal rear lamp clusters, twin reversing lamps, reclining front and individual rear seats, full length centre console, walnut veneer facia with fresh-air vents, servo-assisted brakes (disc at the front), overdrive as standard and a twin-carburettor version of the 1725-cc engine which developed 94 bhp. Automatic transmission was optionally available.

45B: Jaguar 240 Saloon. Appeared in the summer of 1967 as a renamed and revised version of the Mk II 2.4-litre model. Now fitted with a modified cylinder head and dual exhaust system, slimmer bumpers and '240' insignia at the rear. Automatic transmission was optionally available. The Mk II 3.4-litre was also renamed as the '340'.

45C: Lotus Elan S4 FH Coupé. Replacement for the S3, it was distinguishable mainly by a bonnet bulge, large lips on the wheel arches, low profile radial tyres, +2 type rear lamp units and revised interior trim and facia. A DH Coupé version was also available.

45D: Marcos Mini GT 850. This unusual model featured a fibreglass body shell mounted on the sub-frames and suspension, and powered by the engine of the British Leyland Mini.

45E: Marcos 1500. Stylish sports coupé from the Bradford-on-Avon based company Marcos Cars Ltd, which featured a two-door, fibreglass body incorporating a sliding sun-roof, dual headlamps and a luxuriously equipped interior. Engine power came from a Ford, four-cylinder, 1499-cc which developed 85 bhp at 5300 rpm. Also available was the 1600 model with a Ford 1599-cc engine which developed 100 bhp at 5500 rpm.

46A MG 1300 Saloon

46C MG MGC GT Coupé

46B MG MGB Roadster

46D Morgan 4/4 1600 Two-Seater

4/4 4-seater

46E Morgan 4/4 1600 Four-Seater

46B: **MG** MGB Roadster and GT Coupé The Mk II versions of these popular cars featured an all-synchromesh gearbox, an alternator, modified door trims, and on the Roadster reversing lamps as standard. Automatic transmission was optionally available.

46C: **MG** MGC GT Coupé and Roadster. Introduced in the autumn of 1967, this more powerful companion to the MGB featured a six-cylinder, 2912-cc, ohv, seven-bearing crankshaft, 150 bhp engine, servo-assisted brakes, independent torsion bar front suspension and adjustable seat backs. Visible differences from the MGB were a power bulge in the bonnet, a transverse chrome strip and larger wheels. The model never achieved great popularity and it was discontinued in the summer of 1969.

46D/E: **Morgan** 4/4 1600 four-seater Tourer and two-seater Competition replaced the Series V models. Powered by a new Ford 1599-cc. cross-flow head engine which developed 93 bhp at 4750 rpm. A four-seater Competition version was introduced later in the year.

46A: **MG** 1300 Saloon. Introduced in the autumn of 1967, it was of similar appearance to the 1100 which in Mk II form featured a number of changes including 'clipped' tail fins, larger rear lamp clusters and repeater flashers on the front wings. The 1300 version was distinguishable mainly by the 1275-cc, 58 bhp engine (later with twin-carburettors and increased output of 65 bhp), all synchromesh gearbox and '1300' rear designation. Automatic transmission was optionally available. 1100 models were discontinued in the early spring.

47A Morris Mini Mk II Saloon

47B Morris 1800 Mk II Saloon

47C Reliant Rebel Estate Car

47D Reliant Scimitar 2.5-litre

47A: Morris Mini Mk II Saloon. Available in standard and Super de Luxe form, this facelifted model was distinguishable from its predecessor mainly by a new front grille of thirteen horizontal bars, a wider rear window, larger rear lamp clusters, additional brightwork and rear designation. The super de luxe incorporated additional features including carpets, a heater and an oval instrument nacelle. In line with Austin, a Mini 1000 was also introduced and the Mini-Coopers similarly appeared in Mk II form.

47B: Morris 1800 Mk II Saloon. Changes introduced were similar to those on the Austin version but with a slightly different front grille and distinguishing badges. Automatic transmission was optionally available.

47C: Reliant Rebel Estate Car. Introduced in December 1967, this version featured a side-hinged single tailgate and a four-cylinder 701-cc engine which was also now available on the saloon version; the 598-cc engine was discontinued at the beginning of 1968.

47D: Reliant Scimitar 2.5-litre. This fixed head GT Coupé became available as an alternative to the 3-litre version which continued basically unchanged. Externally the two cars were virtually identical apart from the rear designation.

48A Riley Kestrel 1300 Saloon

48B Rolls-Royce Silver Shadow

48C Rover Three Thousand Five Saloon

48D Rover 3.5-litre Coupé

48A: **Riley** Kestrel 1300 Saloon. This model featured the 1275-cc engine developing 58 bhp at 5250 rpm (65 bhp in twin-carburettor form—from March), an all-synchromesh gearbox and detail differences from the 1100, which was released in Mk II form with clipped rear tail fins, larger rear lamp clusters and flashers on the front wings. A Wolseley 1300 Saloon was also available.

48B: **Rolls-Royce** Silver Shadow. Shown is the H. J. Mulliner Park Ward Drophead Coupé which was unveiled in September 1967 and featured a superb specification in keeping with this famous marque, including a power-operated hood. Changes made to the Silver Shadow during the year included stiffened dampers, a rear anti-roll bar on saloons and a three-speed instead of four-speed automatic transmission.

48C: **Rover** Three Thousand Five Saloon. Introduced in the spring, this model was powered by a V-8, 3528-cc, ohv engine developing 184 bhp at 5200 rpm and automatic transmission as standard. It was bodily similar to the '2000' apart from detail differences such as an air intake below the front grille, larger section tyres, rubber-faced overriders, additional brightwork and '3500' and 'V-8' badges. The '2000' was continued with a number of modifications required to meet export specifications.

48D: **Rover** 3.4-litre FH Coupé and Saloon. Powered by a V-8, 3528-cc, ohv, 184 bhp engine and fitted with automatic transmission as standard, these models were generally similar in appearance to the discontinued 3-litre Mk III's apart from detail differences such as special wheels, foglamps, flashers in chrome strips to the rear of the wheel arches, overriders with rubber inserts, twin exhaust tail pipes and insignia front and rear.

49A Sunbeam Stiletto

49C Triumph Herald 13/60 Range

49B Sunbeam Rapier FH Coupé

49D Triumph 1300 TC Saloon

49A: Sunbeam Stiletto FH Coupé. Introduced in the autumn of 1967, it was generally similar in appearance to the Hillman Imp Californian but built to the Sunbeam Sport specification. Distinguishing features included twin-headlamps, black vinyl roof, Amblair upholstery, three-spoke steering wheel and a padded facia incorporating round dials.

49B: Sunbeam Rapier FH Coupé. The familiar shape of the Series V gave way to a new pillarless, two-door fastback model which received a mixed response when it was unveiled in the autumn of 1967. Based mechanically on its predecessor but with overdrive and servo-assisted brakes as standard, the car featured a grille of eight horizontal bars with chrome surround flanked by twin headlamps, a massive, three-piece rear window and twin reversing lights. Automatic transmission was optionally available.

49C: Triumph Herald 13/60. Bodily similar to the Vitesse, but with single headlamps, this replacement for the 12/50 was available in saloon, convertible and estate car form and was powered by the four-cylinder, 1296-cc, ohv engine fitted to the Spitfire and 1300 models.

49D: Triumph 1300 TC Saloon. More powerful version of this front-wheel drive family model which featured a twin-carburettor version of the four-cylinder, 1296-cc engine giving 75 bhp at 6000 rpm, servo-assisted brakes and 'TC' badges front and rear. The basic 1300 saloon continued with minor modifications.

50A Triumph GT6 Mk II Coupé

50B Triumph Vitesse Mk II Convertible

50C Triumph TR5 PI Roadster

50D Triumph 2.5 PI Saloon

50E Vanden Plas 1100 Mk II Saloon

50A: **Triumph** GT6 Mk II FH Coupé. This facelifted sports model featured louvres on the front wings, raised front bumpers, oblong sidelamps, flashers and a chrome extractor grille on the rear quarter panels. Other changes included increased power from the six-cylinder, 2-litre engine, modified rear suspension and a restyled facia. A heater and heated rear window were fitted as standard.

50B: **Triumph** Vitesse Mk II Convertible and Saloon models were announced during the summer although not officially introduced until the autumn. Changes included increased power from the six-cylinder, 2-litre engine, modified rear suspension and a restyled facia. The radiator grille comprising horizontal bars was similar to that of the Herald 13/60.

50C: **Triumph** TR5 PI Roadster and Hardtop Coupé. Although retaining the basic body shape of the superseded TR4A, this powerful newcomer was fitted with a six-cylinder, 2498-cc, ohv, petrol injection engine which developed 150 bhp at 5500 rpm, stiffer rear suspension, more powerful brakes incorporating a fail safe device, and a wooden facia with rocker switches and face-level air vents at each end. Externally the car was distinguishable by its radiator grille or horizontal bars, wider side beading and rear designation. Overdrive was optionally available.

50D: **Triumph** 2.5 PI Saloon. Similar to the 2000 saloon but fitted with a 2498-cc petrol injection engine. Distinguishable primarily by black vinyl rear quarter panels, special wheel trims and 'PI' badges front and rear.

50E: **Vanden Plas** 1100 Mk II Saloon. In line with the MG, Riley and Wolseley variants, this model embraced a number of modifications including clipped tail fins, larger rear light clusters and repeater flashers on the front wings. The new 1300 version was of similar appearance but powered by a 1275-cc, 58 bhp engine driving an all-synchromesh gearbox.

51A Vauxhall Viva SL 1600 Estate Car

51A: **Vauxhall** Viva SL 1600 HB Estate and Saloon Car. Late spring saw the introduction of this more powerful alternative to the standard Viva. The 1599-cc, ohc engine developed 83 bhp at 5600 rpm, and front disc brakes were included in the specification. Externally similar to the standard Viva apart from the rear 'OHC' designation.

51B: **Vauxhall** Viva GT HB Saloon. This high performance addition to the Viva range was powered by a four-cylinder, 1975-cc, ohc, twin-carburettor engine which developed 112 bhp at 5600 rpm. It was distinguishable from other models in the range mainly by twin air scoops on the bonnet, matt black radiator grille, GT badges front and rear and a revised interior which included a black facia with recessed round instrument dials in a padded nacelle, deeper armrests and a full-width parcel shelf. The car also featured front disc brakes, an alternator as standard and a 12-gallon fuel tank.

51B Vauxhall Viva GT HB Saloon

51C Vauxhall Victor 2000 FD Saloon

51C: **Vauxhall** Victor FD Saloon. Continuing their new theme of 'low look body with swept up waistline,' Vauxhall introduced this replacement for the 'FC' in the summer of 1967. Engine power came from the new four-cylinder, 1599-cc, ohc unit—the 1975-cc engine was optionally available—and external features included recessed twin headlamps and horizontal rear lamp clusters. Also available was the 2000 FD Saloon which was generally similar but powered by the 1975-cc engine as standard and fitted with servo-assisted brakes (discs at the front) and an alternator. Estate car versions were introduced during the spring.

51D: **Vauxhall** Victor 3300 FD Estate Car. Featured the same body styling of the other FD models but distinguishable by its radiator grille—as fitted on the new Ventora model—twin exhausts and rear designation. The model featured a six-cylinder, 3294-cc, ohv engine which developed 140 bhp at 4600 rpm and four-speed gearbox with floor change. Automatic transmission, overdrive and leather upholstery were optionally available. Also available was the Vauxhall Ventora FD Saloon, which was essentially a saloon version of the Victor 3300 FD Estate Car, combining the body shell of the new Victor with the six-cylinder, 3.3-litre, ohv engine, and finished to a luxury specification.

51D Vauxhall Victor 3300 FD Estate Car

1969

Many of the models appearing in showrooms for the first time during the year were destined to carry the Industry's challenge well into the coming decade and beyond. Notable among the new arrivals were the Jaguar XJ6, Ford Capri, Austin Maxi, Aston Martin DBS V-8, Morgan Plus Eight, Triumph TR6 PI and the Mini Clubman, the announcement of which coincided with the adoption of 'Mini' as an official British Leyland make name. Also, Lotus released their mid-engined Europa onto the home market. Although production figures were down compared with the previous year, 48% of cars produced were exported, earning the British Motor Industry £350 million at a time when competition from Japan and Continental Europe was greater than ever. Of the 1,717,073 vehicles produced, 892,758 were for the home market and 824,315 for overseas. Sadly, the Riley marque was discontinued during the summer.

52A: **Aston Martin** DB6 Mk II Saloon and Volante Convertible. Appeared in revised form in the summer and included flared wheel arches, six-inch wheels and 8.15 x 15 tyres, power-assisted steering as standard, modified interior layout (similar to the DBS-6 model which was continued basically unchanged) and restyled rear seats. Electronic fuel injection was optionally available.

52B: **Aston Martin** DBS V-8 Sports Saloon. Announced in the summer, this powerful new sporting model was powered by a V-8, 5340-cc, ohc engine and featured mechanical fuel injection and power-assisted steering. Bodily similar to the DBS-6 but distinguishable mainly by alloy wheels and vent outlets below the rear window. Price £6897.

52C: **Austin** 1300 GT Saloon. Four-door, sporting version of this popular front-wheel drive model which was unveiled in the autumn and featured a twin-carburettor, 70 bhp version of the 1275-cc engine. Visible differences included a mesh black grille, black vinyl roof, chrome waistline strip, GT badges front and rear, matt black facia with three circular dials including a rev. counter, special steering wheel and reclining front seats as standard. Morris version was also available. Other 1300 models continued unchanged.

52A Aston Martin DB6 Mk II Saloon

52B Aston Martin DBS V-8 Saloon

52C Austin 1300 GT Saloon

53A Austin Maxi Saloon

53B Austin 1800 'S' De Luxe Saloon

53C Bond Equipe 2-litre GT Mk II Saloon

53A: Austin Maxi Saloon. Spring saw the arrival of this new family model which filled the gap between the 1300 and 1800 ranges. Featuring four conventional doors and an opening rear door which gave access to generous luggage space, or alternatively, a 'double-bed' arrangement with the seats folded flat, this front-wheel drive model combined the advantages of an estate car with the general appearance of a saloon. It was powered by a transversely mounted, 1485-cc, ohc, 74 bhp engine and was fitted with a five-speed all-synchromesh gearbox, Hydrolastic suspension and servo-assisted front disc brakes. Price £979.

53B: Austin 1800 'S' De Luxe Saloon. This high performance version of the popular 1800 model was fitted with a twin-carburettor version of the 1798-cc, front-wheel drive engine which developed 97 bhp at 5700 rpm and more powerful brakes, and was externally recognizable by the boot-mounted 'S' designation. Initially available in manual form only; automatic transmission became optionally available later in the year.

53C: Bond Equipe 2-litre GT Sports Saloon. The Mk II version of this Vitesse based model incorporated a number of changes including modified rear suspension, increased power from the 1998-cc engine, magnum wheel trims and a restyled facia. Also introduced was a convertible version which despite its appearance offered four-seat accommodation and an integral 'hideaway' hood. During the year Bond's interests were acquired by the Reliant Company, but this change did not immediately affect either company's model ranges.

53D Daimler Limousine

53D: Daimler Limousine. The eight-seater, luxury model was coachbuilt by Vanden Plas and featured the traditional Daimler front and semi-razor edge rear-end styling. Its impressive standard specification included the six-cylinder, 4.2-litre, ohc engine, automatic transmission, power-assisted steering, all-independent suspension and disc brakes all round. The price of £3827 was certainly inexpensive for a car designed to be chauffeur driven.

54A Ford Escort Super Saloon

54B Ford Escort GT Saloon

54A: **Ford** Escort Super Saloon. Added to the range in the autumn of 1968, this model, available with both the 1100 and 1300 engines, featured revised door trim, additional brightwork and a wood finished instrument panel. Estate car versions were also available. Four-door versions of the standard, de luxe and super models were introduced later in the year.

54B: **Ford** Escort GT Saloon. This two-door sporting model featured new fittings introduced on the Super Saloon but with the addition of a matt black front grille and wood cappings on the doors and rear quarter panels. A four-door version was introduced later in the year. The Escort Twin Cam also received a number of detail modifications.

54C: **Ford** Cortina Saloon. Modifications made to this fast-selling model included black detail paint treatment to the front grille, revised gearbox and remote control lever, and new Ford lettering on bonnet and boot lid. Available in two- and four-door saloon and estate car versions with either a 1300 or 1600 engine. The two-door 1600 model was discontinued. Super and GT models were similarly modified, and in addition super models were given restyled front seats and the GT model a revised centre console with floor-mounted handbrake, and gauges incorporated into the facia proper.

54C Ford Cortina Saloon

55A Ford Capri 1600 XL Saloon

55B Ford Capri 2000 GT Saloon

55A: **Ford** Capri Saloon. Ford Europe Inc. announced their much publicized new sports saloon at the beginning of the year. Based generally on the lines of the American Mustang, the development of the two-door fastback model (code name 'Colt') was a combined operation between Ford of Dagenham and Ford Germany which resulted in an attractive four-seater capable of accepting various Ford engines and three optional trim packs ('X', 'L' and 'R'). Initially available with 1298-cc and 1599-cc engines in both standard and GT form (52, 64, 64 and 82 bhp, respectively) the range was increased subsequently with the announcement of 2000 GT and 3000 GT versions. The optional trim packs included reclining front seats, sculptured road wheels, fog and spot lamps, dummy air scoops, sports steering wheel and matt black bonnet and tail panel, according to specification.

55B: **Ford** Capri 2000 GT Saloon. This addition to the Capri range, which was introduced during the spring, was fitted with a V-4 1996-cc engine developing 93 bhp at 5500 rpm. Otherwise it was similar to the 1600 GT model. A 3000 GT model powered by a V-6, 2994-cc engine was added to the range at the end of the year.

55C: **Ford** Zephyr, Zodiac and Executive Saloons were continued with detail changes including a padded steering wheel and new Ford lettering on the bonnet and boot lid. The estate car versions were similarly modified. Towards the end of the year all models were given a revised suspension system; Zodiac and Executive versions also received additional brightwork, walnut facia (walnut finish extended across whole facia and door cappings on Executive models), restyled front seats and heated rear window as standard.

55C Ford Zephyr Four Mk IV De Luxe Saloon

56A: **Ginetta** G15 Sports. Powered by the Sunbeam Sport, 875-cc engine developing 55 bhp at 6100 rpm, this attractive and well-equipped little two-seater coupé had impressive performance which gave it a top speed in excess of 100 mph. When it was first announced, Ginetta was faced with something of a problem as the demand for the G15 was considerable and production facilities were limited.

56B: **Hillman** Imp Saloon. Facelifted version introduced onto the market in the autumn of 1968. Changes included a restyled front, revised facia incorporating round dials, padded steering wheel spokes, modified stalk switch arrangement, restyled seating, front aluminium panel (except de luxe version) and rear aluminium panel and a glove box in the facia (super model only). The Californian FH Coupé and Husky Estate Car were similarly modified. The Mk II designation was discontinued.

56C: **Hillman** Minx De Luxe Saloon. This addition to the 'Hunter' bodied range was distinguishable by additional brightwork, 'De Luxe' on the boot lid, a centre console and a matt black facia, and was fully carpeted. A Hunter GT model increased the range further at the end of the year.

56D: **Jaguar** XJ6 2.8-litre Saloon. Introduced amidst a blaze of publicity in the summer of 1968, this impressive newcomer featured a low profile, wide-based, four-door body with a rectangular front grille, twin headlamps and slim pillars which gave a large glass area and excellent all-round visibility. The specification included a new version of the six-cylinder, 2.8 litre, twin ohc, XK engine which developed 180 bhp at 6000 rpm, four-speed all synchromesh gearbox, dual circuit servo-assisted brakes, power-assisted steering (standard on de luxe version), traditional Jaguar facia layout, and luxuriously appointed interior, including leather upholstery on de luxe models. Overdrive and automatic transmission were optionally available. A 4.2-litre engined version was also available.

56A Ginetta G15

56B Hillman Imp De Luxe Saloon

56C Hillman Minx De Luxe Saloon

56D Jaguar XJ6 2.8-litre Saloon

57A: Jaguar 'E' Type Open Two-Seater and FH Coupé Series 2 models (background) were announced in the autumn of 1968. New features included wrap-around bumpers, larger headlamps positioned further forward, enlarged rear lamp and front side/flasher units, twin reversing lights, reshaped front air intake and a revised interior which included improved safety features such as an energy-absorbing steering column, recessed switches and hazard warning lights, reclining front seats and a modified windscreen wiper motor.

Jaguar 'E' Type FH Coupé 2 + 2 Series 2 (foreground) was continued with changes similar to those featured on companion 'E' Types, and, in addition, the introduction of a windscreen with an increased angle of rake. Power-assisted steering was optionally available on all 'E' Type models.

57B: Jensen Interceptor Mk II Saloon, which replaced the Mk I in the autumn, featured a number of changes such as a relocated front bumper, square overriders, black headlamp surrounds and widely spaced bars in the side air intakes. Interior refinements included built-in headrests, a restyled instrument nacelle and a single row of rocker switches.

57C: Lotus Europa S2 (Series 54) FH Coupé. Following its introduction on overseas markets during 1967/68, this unusual sports model appeared in UK showrooms during the summer of 1969. The first mid-engined British coupé to be produced for road use, its 1470-cc engine and transmission were produced in association with the French Renault organization. The fibreglass body, which included recessed headlamps, a vertical rear window and large fins extending from the roof line to the rear, was designed by John Frayling and mounted on a backbone chassis similar to that of the Elan.

57A Jaguar 'E' Type Series 2

57B Jensen Interceptor Mk II Saloon

57C Lotus Europe S2 FH Coupé

58A Lotus Elan Plus 2S FH Coupé

58C MG 1300 Mk II Saloon

58B MG Midget Mk III Sports

58D MG MGB Roadster

58A: **Lotus** Elan Plus 2S FH Coupé. This attractive model, which was announced in the autumn of 1968, was powered by the 1558-cc, twin-cam engine producing 118 bhp. It was similar to the Plus 2 but featured a de luxe interior. The Plus 2 FH Coupé was discontinued at the end of the year.

58B: **MG** Midget Sports (Series G/AN 5). The Mk III Midget in its facelifted form was recognizable by a matt black radiator grille with chrome trim and surround and a centrally mounted 'MG' badge, black sills with chrome strips and 'MIDGET' lettering, twin rear quarter bumpers and modified front seats. The Austin-Healey Sprite Mk IV model was built to a similar specification.

58C: **MG** 1300 Mk II Saloon. This two-door model was now powered by a 70 bhp version of the 1275-cc engine which featured twin SU HS2 carburettors. Other significant changes included a more luxurious interior incorporating walnut facia panel and three large circular instruments, rocker switches, an attractive leather-rimmed steering wheel and redesigned and retrimmed seats. Maximum speed was up to 95 mph. The Riley version was similarly modified.

58D: **MG** MGB Sports Roadster (Series GHN 5) and FH Coupé GT (Series GHD 5). Facelifted versions of this popular range were announced in the autumn and featured a matt black vertical bar radiator grille with chrome trim and surround and 'MG' badge mounted centrally, new perforated spoke steering wheel, revised trim and reclining front seats.

59A Mini 850 Saloon

59B Mini Clubman Saloon

59C Morgan Plus 8 Sports

59D Morris 1800 'S' De Luxe Saloon

59A: Mini 850 Saloon. Austin and Morris versions were no longer available and 'Mini' was now officially classed as a make name. First produced in August although not officially announced until the autumn, this modified model featured dry cone suspension in place of the Hydrolastic type, larger doors with concealed hinges and wind-up windows and new badges front and rear. A Mini 1000 (998-cc engine) saloon was also available and visibly distinguishable mainly by different badges and rear opening quarter lights.

59B: Mini Clubman Saloon and Estate Car. Unmistakably a Mini but with a modified front end comprising a larger bonnet, full-width black mesh grille and chrome trim. Powered by the 998-cc, front wheel drive, transverse engine, this model featured Hydrolastic suspension and a better equipped interior than the Mini. The Estate Car version which was fitted with double rear doors had simulated wood strips on the sides and at the rear. Respective lengths of the saloon and estate car were 10 ft 4½ in and 11 ft 2 in. The Mini 1275 GT Saloon was similar to the Clubman but powered by a four-cylinder, 1275-cc, engine.

59C: Morgan Plus 8 Sports. October 1968 saw the arrival of the Malvern based Company's powerful new open two-seater. Engine power came from the Rover V-8, 3528-cc, ohv aluminium unit which developed 184 bhp at 5200 rpm, and was housed under the bonnet of a conventionally spartan Morgan body mounted on a stiffened and extended chassis frame. Externally the Plus 8 was distinguishable from other Morgans primarily by its distinctive cast aluminium wheels. The cockpit featured bucket seats and a vinyl covered facia with recessed rocker switches. Price £1510.

59D: Morris 1800 'S' De Luxe Saloon. Externally similar to the Mk II 1800 De Luxe, apart from the boot-mounted 'S' designation, but fitted with a 100 bhp, twin-carburettor version of the 1798-cc engine, modified choke control and larger brakes. The model was initially available only with manual transmission, however, automatic transmission became optional in the summer.

60A Reliant Scimitar FH GT Coupé

60B Reliant Scimitar FH GTE Coupé

60C Rolls-Royce Silver Shadow lwb Saloon

60D Rolls-Royce Phantom VI Limousine

60A: Reliant Scimitar FH GT Coupé. Changes made to the V-6, 3.0-litre engined, two-door model included a revised interior featuring leathercloth covering on centre console and tunnel, modified seating, multi-function control switch and a repositioned interior lamp. The 2.5-litre engined model was similarly modified. Both models were discontinued towards the end of 1970.

60B: Reliant Scimitar FH GTE Coupé. A development of the GT model, this impressive newcomer known as the SE5 Series won enthusiastic acclaim for its highly attractive Ogle designed fibreglass bodywork which was both stylish and functional. The large opening rear 'door cum window' gave access to 36 cu. ft of space with the occasional rear seat folded flat. Although fitted with the 3-litre engine and four-speed synchromesh gearbox of the GT model, the revised chassis gave the GTE a longer wheelbase and wider track and the suspension was improved in line with the increased weight. Top speed of this versatile coupé/estate was in excess of 110 mph. Price £1759.

60C: Rolls-Royce Silver Shadow Long-wheelbase Saloon. This luxurious version was introduced onto the United States market in the spring and onto the UK market in the autumn. New features included a vinyl covered roof, small rear window and separate air-conditioning units front and rear. A division was optionally available. The standard and two-door saloons and convertible (previously known as the DH Coupé) models were also modified to bring them into line with US Federal Safety Regulations.

60D: Rolls-Royce Phantom VI Limousine. This massive H. J. Mulliner Park Ward model replaced the Phantom V in the autumn of 1968. Changes included refrigeration as standard, front and rear, and wool twill upholstery. Overall length was 19 ft 10 in, and it was the most expensive Rolls-Bentley model at £13,123.

61A: **Singer** Chamois Sport Saloon and FH Coupé. Changes made during the autumn of 1968 included a restyled front end featuring twin headlamps and narrower dummy grille, new seating, full-width facia panel with circular instrumentation, new steering wheel and redesigned heating/ ventilation controls. Both models were discontinued in 1970 when the Singer name was phased out; the Sport was continued, however, under the Sunbeam banner.

61B: **Sunbeam** Imp Sport Saloon. Some two years after its introduction this model received a number of modifications including a front end aluminium panel, revised facia and a steering wheel with padded spokes. It was discontinued in the spring of 1970 and replaced by the Sport Saloon, which was basically the discontinued Singer Chamois Sport with Sunbeam badges.

61C: **Sunbeam** Alpine FH Coupé. Although bodily the same as the Rapier and H120 models, apart from brightwork, fittings, badges etc., this four-seater model, which was unveiled in the autumn, was powered by a single carburettor version of the 1725-cc engine which developed 74 bhp. Distinguishing features were the twin chrome strips across the boot and the high back front seats.

61D: **Sunbeam** H 120 FH Coupé. High performance version of the pillarless fastback bodied Rapier. Differences included greater engine power, (105 bhp at 5200 rpm) and distinguishing body features such as a black radiator grille, tail spoiler, twin body side stripes, sports wheels and 'H 120' badges. The Rapier model continued unchanged.

61A Singer Chamois Sport

61B Sunbeam Imp Sport

61C Sunbeam Alpine Coupé

61D Sunbeam H120 Coupé

62A: **Triumph** TR6 PI, available in Roadster and Hardtop Coupé versions, was largely a facelifted version of the superseded TR5 PI as, apart from a modified suspension system, the technical specification remained essentially the same. Visible differences included a recessed black radiator grille, double horizontal chrome bars with central badge across the oval front aperture, a square rear end with wrap around horizontal lamp clusters, and restyled seats. A matt black window surround, reclining front seats and satin chrome steering wheel spokes were introduced later in the year.

62B: **Triumph** 2000 Mk II Saloon. This facelifted version, introduced in the autumn, was distinguishable from its predecessor by its more streamlined front end styling which featured a longer and lower bonnet with full-width horizontal bar radiator grille and dual headlamps, a larger boot and horizontal rear lamp clusters. Other changes included a full-width wood finish facia and an alternator instead of a generator. The estate car version received similar changes, as did the 2.5 PI models which were distinguishable mainly by the matt black radiator grille and rear panel.

62C: **TVR** Vixen S2. This GT Coupé was bodily similar to the Grantura 1800 model (first introduced in 1963) but powered by a Ford, four-cylinder, 1599-cc engine developing 92 bhp at 5500 rpm, with a four-speed, all-synchromesh gearbox. The two-door fibreglass body was mounted on a tubular space-frame chassis. Price £1583.

62D: **Unipower** GT. This sleek, Mini-based model from Universal Power Drives Ltd, which was first announced in 1966, was powered by a rear-mounted, 998-cc Cooper engine and featured a two-door, two-seater fibreglass body mounted on a tubular space-frame chassis.

62A Triumph TR6 PI Roadster

62B Triumph 2000 Mk II Saloon

62C TVR Vixen S2

62D Unipower GT

63A: **Vauxhall** Viva Saloon. Four-door variants of this family model were introduced in the autumn of 1968, available in de luxe and '90', de luxe 1600, SL and '90' and SL 1600 versions, with either manual or automatic transmission. The two-door versions were continued with a number of modifications including repositioned switches on the facia, revised door trim and a full-width parcel shelf. The capacity of the fuel tank on 1600 models was increased from 8 to 12 gallons.

63B: **Vauxhall** VX 4/90 Saloon. Late summer saw the arrival of this new medium range, four-door model which was generally similar to the Ventora but was powered by a four-cylinder, 1975-cc, ohv, 104 bhp engine.

63C: **Vauxhall** Ventora Mk II Saloon. Changes introduced on this later version included bright sill mouldings, 'Ventora II' boot designation, restyled facia, twin spoke aluminium steering wheel, reclining front seats and two-speed windscreen wipers.

63D: **Wolseley** 1300 Saloon. In Mk II form this four-door, front wheel drive model featured increased output from its 1275-cc engine and included a number of detail changes such as folding armrest between rear seats, rocker switches on the facia, additional external brightwork and a boot-mounted model designation.

63E: **Wolseley** 18/85 Mk II Saloon. Improvements made on this version were concentrated on the interior fittings and controls and included larger walnut door cappings, folding armrest between deeper front seats, restyled front door pockets and rocker switches in place of the toggle type. The Mk II 'S' model introduced later in the year was powered by a twin-carburettor, 97 bhp version of the 1798-cc engine and was distinguishable by a chrome waistline body strip and the boot-mounted 'S' designation.

63A Vauxhall Viva Saloon

63B Vauxhall VX 4/90 Saloon

63C Vauxhall Ventora Mk II Saloon

63D Wolseley 1300 Mk II Saloon

63E Wolseley 18/85 Mk II Saloon

INDEX OF MANUFACTURERS

SUMMARY OF MAJOR BRITISH CAR MAKES
1965–69 (with dates of their existence)

AC	(from 1908)	MG	(from 1924–81)
Alvis	(1920–67)	Morgan	(from 1910)
Aston Martin	(from 1922)	Morris	(from 1913)
Austin	(from 1906)		
		Riley	(1898–1969)
Bentley	(from 1920)	Rolls-Royce	(from 1904)
Bristol	(from 1947)	Rover	(from 1904)
Daimler	(from 1896)	Singer	(1905–70)
		Sunbeam	(1953–76)
Ford	(from 1911)		
		Triumph	(from 1953)
Hillman	(1907–76)		
Humber	(1898–1976)	Vauxhall	(from 1903)
Jaguar	(from 1932)	Wolseley	(1911–76)
Lotus	(from 1952)		

ABBREVIATIONS

bhp	brake horse power
cc	cubic centimetres (engine capacity)
mpg	miles per gallon
mph	miles per hour
ohc	overhead camshaft (engine)
ohv	overhead valve (engine)
rpm	revolutions per minute

ACKNOWLEDGEMENTS

This book was compiled largely from historic source material in the library of the Olyslager Organisation. Grateful thanks are extended to John Weston Hays for his help in locating research material and to Dawn Voller for her valuable assistance in preparing the text.